MAGNA C

By

Daphne I. Stroud, M.A.

With an English translation from the Latin text based on W. S. McKechnie, "Magna Carta" (1914).

Published by Paul Cave Publications Ltd., 74 Bedford Place, Southampton
In association with the Dean and Chapter of Salisbury.

Printed by Shearprint, Unit 3a, Vickers Business Park, Priestley Road, Basingstoke, Hampshire, RG24 9NP

Published July, 1980
Reprinted August, 1980
Reprinted May, 1981
Reprinted August, 1982
Reprinted October, 1983
Reprinted November, 1984
Reprinted August, 1985
Reprinted June, 1986
Reprinted July, 1987
Reprinted June, 1988
Reprinted July, 1989
Reprinted June, 1990
Reprinted June, 1992
Reprinted June, 1993
Reprinted June, 1994
Reprinted June, 1996
Reprinted February, 1997
Reprinted September, 1997
Reprinted July, 1998

ISBN 0-86146-012-X

Front Cover designed by Harry Stevens.

MAGNA CARTA

In the early summer of 1215 a party of barons from the northern and eastern shires of England rose in revolt against King John. Their grievances were of long standing; John's wars, fought to retain and then to recover the continental possessions of the house of Plantagenet, had been a constant drain on the wealth of the country, and his methods of raising the revenue he needed caused bitter resentment. The fines and dues payable under feudal tenure were set at arbitary and extortionate rates; men were imprisoned, their lands seized and pillaged, for failure to pay.

John's continental campaign of 1214 had led to defeat at Bouvines, and with this disaster had ended all hope of recovering Normandy for the English crown. The financial exactions for this expedition had been particularly harsh, but the victims had at least the prospect of recouping their losses from the spoils of victory; after Bouvines there was nothing to prevent the discontent at home breaking out into active rebellion. The barons who had suffered most were determined to secure themselves against future infringements of their 'liberties' — their right to enjoy their lands and property without arbitary interference. They wanted a pledge that John would be powerless to break, and they were prepared to go to war to secure it.

In January 1215, John was at the Temple in London when a group of the northern barons presented themselves in arms, and demanded the grant of a charter confirming the ancient 'liberties' of the realm. John temporised, putting off an answer until a meeting to be held at Northampton at the end of April. The barons came to the meeting prepared for war, and when John failed to appear they renounced their fealty and homage.

Thereafter events moved quickly. On 17 May the barons, with the connivance of some of the citizens, seized the city of London; with the rebels holding his capital and the Exchequer, John could no longer rely on tactics of delay and evasion.

The barons' demands were formulated in greater detail and set out in a document known as 'The Articles of the Barons' (now in the British Library) which covered the main points finally incorporated in Magna Carta. The Archbishop of Canterbury, Stephen Langton, who acted as intermediary in the negotiations, used his influence to press for a settlement, and John capitulated. The rebels were by this time encamped at Staines, while the King and his supporters were in the royal castle of Windsor. Half way between, 'in the meadow which is called Runnymede', the two parties met on 15 June and John, no doubt with suitably imposing ceremonial, made a formal grant of the 'liberties' which he had conceded. Letters were then issued to sheriffs and bishops throughout the country informing them briefly of the terms on which peace had been concluded, copies of Magna Carta were prepared for distribution, and the barons renewed their homage.

The importance of Magna Carta

With the issue of Magna Carta at Runnymede the demands of a few malcontents for the redress of personal grievances, and for a vaguely-worded promise of protection from further injustices, were transformed into a charter of exact and detailed rights; a document which formulated the aspirations of the best men of the period so effectively that generation after generation sought the guarantee of their own rights through the reaffirmation of its principal provisions.

Much of the credit for this achievement must be ascribed to Stephen Langton, a man of outstanding ability and wide experience, who had been a distinguished theologian and canon lawyer before becoming archbishop of Canterbury, Langton had returned to England in 1213 after a long exile during the King's quarrel with the Pope, and had immediately demanded a reaffirmation of John's coronation oath guaranteeing the 'liberties' of the Church. His stand on the rights of the Church made him a natural leader in the parallel movement for definition of the rights of the secular barons. He took a leading role in the negotiations for the charter, and was one of the principal participants in the ceremony at Runnymede. Under his influence Magna Carta in its final form clearly embodied the principle that the King was bound by law in the exercise of his power, and that the same law in turn bound the barons in the exercise of theirs, and so gave protection, not just to the few, but to all 'free men'.

4

The essence of Magna Carta's achievement can be seen in three of its most famous clauses, where John promised:

> "No free man shall be taken or imprisoned or disseised or outlawed or exiled or in any way ruined, nor will we go or send against him, except by the lawful judgement of his peers or by the law of the land. To no one will we sell, to no one will we deny or delay right or justice . . . .

> "Moreover, all those aforesaid customs and liberties, the observance of which we have granted in our kingdom as far as pertains to us towards our men, shall be observed by all our kingdom, as well clergy as laymen, as far as pertains to them towards their men."

The peace which had been concluded at Runnymede and sealed by the issue of Magna Carta did not last. Soon after the meeting broke up John wrote to the Pope asking to be released from his undertakings, on the grounds that they had been exacted under duress. The Pope's reply, granting such release, probably reached England by the end of September. The barons on their side never gave up their principal bargaining counter, the city of London. In October the war broke out again, and continued until John's death from dysentery at Newark in October, 1216.

Once the much-hated John was dead the great barons of the realm rallied to his son Henry, then a child of nine. Magna Carta, its temporary provisions dropped, was re-issued as the young King's coronation charter, and in the following year the civil war ended with the submission of the remaining rebels.

Throughout the rest of the thirteenth century demands for the re-issue of Magna Carta provided a constantly recurring motif in the history of the struggles between king and barons. Six re-issues, with appropriate amendments, were granted and the last — Edward I's confirmation of 1297 — was in due course placed on the Statute Book, and became part of the law of the land.

Many of the detailed provisions of Magna Carta relating to feudal rights and dues fell into disuse in the course of time. On the other hand, as the originally limited class of 'free men' expanded to include every citizen, the remaining clauses became of general application. When, under the Stuarts in the seventeenth century, Englishmen were again seeking

(continued on page 8)

Opposite: *Part of the Salisbury Magna Carta (actual size).*
This reproduction shows the bottom right-hand corner of the
document. The last line (with the abbreviations expanded)
reads in Latin: "Testibus Supradictis et multis aliis. Data per
manum nostram in prato quod vocatur Runingmed inter
Windesore et Stane."
"Witness the above-mentioned and many others. Given under
our hand in the meadow which is called Runnymede between
Windsor and Staines."

...tra cont nos gwerrina. 7 si uri salui sint ibi. alu salui sint i tra nra. Liceat unicuiq; de cro exire de
...r sctm lege regni. 7 genre de tra cont nos gwerrina. 7 mcatorib; de quib; fiat su pdictm est. Siqs tenuit
ad Relenui nec fueit nob aliud seruiciu qm fac. 7 Baroni si Baronia illa ee i manu Baronis. nos ecc
t plegii alicui ut aliquoz q attachiati sunt p foresta. Nos n faciem Justiciarios ut Constabularios. Vicecom
nra. Habet earu custodia cu uacauerint sic hre debent. Oms foreste q afforestate sr tempe nro stati deafforestet
iustit. Rapariis. 7 earu custodib; statim inqiratur in quolibet Comitatu p duodecim milites iuratos de eodem
Choc seiam. pris ut Justiciari ur si nos in Anglia n fuim. Oms obsides. 7 cartas statim reddem q libate dieit
Engelendu de Cigonu. Andream. Petru. 7 Gyone de Chancell. Gyone de Cigonu. Galfridu de atarrem. 7 fre
os. Seruientes. Supendiarios q uenent cu eqs. 7 armis ad nocumtm Regni. Siqs fuit dissetsiat ut elongat
iqnq; Baronu de quib; sit mentio inferi i securitate pacis. De omnib; au illis de quib; aliqd dissetsit fuit uel
inrumare. respectu hebim usq; ad comune tmin cruce signatoz. Exceptis illis de qb; placitm motu fuit ut
inde au respectu hebimus. 7 code modo de Justicia exhibenda de forestis deafforestandis ut remansuris forestis
cu militare. 7 de Abbatis q fundare fuerit in feodo alti qm nro in qb; dns feodi dixerit se ius hre. 7 cu redieri
n uerit sui. Oms fines q iniuste 7 cont lege tre facti sunt nobcu. 7 omia Amciamta tra iniuste 7 cont lege tre
o Cantuar Archiepo si itee pot. 7 Alus qs secu ad hoc uocare uoluit. Et si itee n pot. nichomin pcedat
hoc faciend elect. 7 uitan substituat. Si nos dissetsiuim ut elongauim Walenses de tris ut libatatib; ut rob;
mus Anglie. scdm lege Anglie. De tenentis Wallie. scdm lege Wallie. De tenentis marchie. scdm legi mar
Rege frem nrm q nos in manu nra habem ut que Alu tenent q nos oportet Warantizare. respectum
mu et si fere remanserim a pregnatione nra statim eis inde plena iusticia exhibebim scdm lege Wallie.
7 de sororibz suis. 7 obsidib; reddendis. 7 libatatib; suis. 7 iure suo scdm forma in q faciem Alus Baronib; nris
ictas. 7 libatates qs nos concessim in Regno nro tenendas qntu ad nos ptinet erga nros. oms de Regno nro
omia pdicta concesserint. uoluerit ea firma. 7 integ stabilitate gaude imppetuu. faciem. 7 concedim eis secu
qs eis concessim. 7 hac pstem carta nra confirmauim. Ita scilicet qd si nos ut Justiciari nr ut Balli nri ut aliqs
illi qruos Barones accedent ad nos ut ad Justiciariu nrm si fuim ext Regnu pponentes nob crassu. 7 peirit ut ea
nonstrari fuit nob ut Justiciarius nris si ext Regnu fuim. pdich. iiij. Barones referant cam illam ad residu
alis quib; potit dni fuit emdari. scdm arbitriu eoz. Salua psona nra. 7 regine nre. 7 libou nroz. Et cu fuerit
publice. 7 libe datu licencia iurandi cuilibet q iurare uoluit. 7 nulla unqm uetitu phibebim. Oms au illos de tra
nonib; decesserit ut a tra recesserit ut aliq alio modo impedit fuit q mir ista pdicta possent creqi qui residui fue
psentes fuim. 7 nir se sup re Aliqua discordauit ut aliq ex ex suionu noluit ut neqiut itee. Ratu tamen
obseruari. Et nos nich imperabim ab alio p nos. ut p aliu p qd Aliq istar concessionu. 7 libatatu reuocet ut mi
ut. 7 Laicos a tmpe discordie. plene omnib; remisim. 7 condonamus. Preta oms tsgressiones factas ocone eiusde
fieri litras testimoniales patentes dni Stephi Cantuar Archiepi. 7 Gifom pdictoz. 7 magri Pandulfi sup secu
7 concessiones oms bn in pace. libe. 7 quiete plene. 7 intege sibi. 7 hedib; suis de nob. 7 heredib; nris in omnib;
Testib; supradictis. 7 mutis Alus. Dat p manu nram in pto qd uocatur Runingmed int Windesor. 7 Stane

7

means to control what appeared to them the tyranny of an absolute monarch, they turned to Magna Carta as a basic statement of the primacy of the rule of law over the power of the Crown.

Five hundred and sixty-one years after the meeting at Runnymede, and more than three thousand miles, away, another group of rebels, fighting to establish a free and independent state in which the law would provide a lasting defence against oppression, embodied the concepts of Magna Carta, and even echoed its phrases, in their Declaration of Independence, and ultimately in the Constitution of the United States of America.

The Salisbury Exemplification

Four exemplifications (attested copies under seal) of the text of King John's Magna Carta have survived. Two (one of which has been badly damaged by fire and is illegible) are now in the British Library, one in Lincoln Cathedral, and one at Salisbury. All four are of equal validity, and none is "the original Magna Carta" in the sense that it and no other figured in the ceremony at Runnymede. At this ceremony John bound himself by public oath before witnesses; the exemplifications of the charter were intended to record the undertakings so given, and to publish them to the rest of the realm. In the event it seems unlikely that a full distribution to all sheriffs and bishops ever took place. Evidence survives for the issues of only thirteen exemplifications; seven issued from Runnymede on or soon after 24 June, and six more (of which Salisbury's was probably one) from Oxford on 22 July.

The Salisbury exemplification is written on a single skin of vellum measuring 14 by 17¼ inches; the text consists of 76 lines running parallel to the shorter sides. It is in Latin, the language of all official documents of the period, written with the standard medieval time and space-saving abbreviations. It was sealed, not signed; sealing was the normal method of authenticating a document at the time. The seal is missing but the eyelet-holes, through which the cord originally holding it would have been threaded, can still be seen.

A fourteenth century press-mark on the back of the document indicates that it was at that period kept in the first press of cupboard of the muniment room of the Cathedral. It is known to have been in the Cathedral in the seventeenth century but was apparently missing by the early eighteenth,

*King John's Seal (photo-
graphs: Public Record
Office, London).*

9

and was not found again until about 1814. It was duly recorded when the first modern inventory of the muniment room was made in 1875.

Two men of Salisbury

Two outstanding men who had close connections with Salisbury took a direct part in the events of 1215.

William Longspee, Earl of Salisbury and Sheriff of Wiltshire, was an illegitimate son of Henry II (and thus a half-brother of King John), a leading baron of the realm, and one of John's principal military commanders. His name appears in the preamble to Magna Carta, in the list of prominent men on whose advice the grant was made. He was almost certainly not at the Runnymede ceremony as he was campaigning against the rebels near Exeter at the time, but John may well have consulted him during the earlier stages of the negotiations.

Longspee, a loyal servant of his young nephew Henry III, survived his brother by ten years. He and his wife, Ela, were present, as the principal patrons, at the laying of the foundation stones of Salisbury Cathedral in 1220. He died at Old Sarum castle in 1226, after a short illness, and was the first person to be buried in the newly-completed Lady Chapel. His fine tomb and effigy are now in the south aisle of the nave.

Elias of Dereham, the second Salisbury personality, was more closely involved. Elias was for many years in the service of Hubert Walter (Archbishop of Canterbury 1193-1205) and after the latter's death joined the household of Stephen Langton. In 1215 he was Langton's steward and in that capacity acted as his right-hand man in the negotiations for the charter. He may possibly have been the "canon from Dereham" who, according to one chronicler, carried the barons' formal renunciation of their fealty from their camp at Brackley in Northamptonshire to King John at Wallingford certainly he was present at Runnymede and four of the seven copies of Magna Carta issued there were handed to him for delivery, together with a number of royal writs dealing with the agreement; all six copies issued at Oxford were given to him for distribution. When Langton went to Rome in the autumn of 1215, Elias remained in London with the main body of rebels; he identified himself with their cause to such

Opposite: *Effigy of William Longspee, Earl of Salisbury, in Salisbury Cathedral.*

10

11

A 17th century drawing of King John's tomb in Worcester Cathedral.

an extent that, when in 1217 the Treaty of Kingston brought the civil war to an end, he was one of the three clerics exempted from the general amnesty and banished abroad. A few years later, however, he obtained a papal pardon and returned to England to become a resident canon of Salisbury, and to supervise the building of the new cathedral.

Elias has no monument, but a man who played a major part both in the issue of Magna Carta and in the building of Salisbury Cathedral, surely needs no other memorial.

12

MAGNA CARTA

TRANSLATION

John, by the grace of God, king of England, lord of Ireland, duke of Normandy and Aquitaine, and count of Anjou, to the archbishops, bishops, abbots, earls, barons, justiciars, foresters, sheriffs, stewards, servants, and to all his bailiffs and liege subjects, greeting. Know that, having regard to God and for the salvation of our soul, and those of all our ancestors and heirs, and unto the honour of God and the advancement of holy Church, and for the reform of our realm, by advice of our venerable fathers, Stephen, archbishop of Canterbury, primate of all England and cardinal of the holy Roman Church, Henry archbishop of Dublin, William of London, Peter of Winchester, Jocelyn of Bath and Glastonbury, Hugh of Lincoln, Walter of Worcester, William of Coventry, Benedict of Rochester, bishops; of master Pandulf, subdeacon and member of the household of our lord the Pope, of brother Aymeric (master of the Knights of the Temple in England), and of the illustrious men William Marshal, earl of Pembroke, William, earl of Salisbury, William, earl Warenne, William, earl of Arundel, Alan of Galloway (constable of Scotland), Waren Fitz Gerald, Hubert de Burgh (seneschal of Poitou), Peter Fitz Herbert, Hugh de Neville, Matthew Fitz Herbert, Thomas Basset, Alan Basset, Philip d'Aubigny, Robert of Roppesley, John Marshal, John Fitz Hugh, and others, our liegemen.

In the first place we have granted to God, and by this our present charter confirmed for us and our heirs for ever that the English church shall be free, and shall have her rights entire, and her liberties inviolate; and we will that it be thus observed; which is apparent from this that the freedom of elections, which is reckoned most important and very essential to the English church, we, of our pure and unconstrained will, did grant, and did by our charter confirm and did obtain the ratification of the same from our lord. Pope Innocent III, before the quarrel arose between us and our barons: and this we will observe, and our will is that it be observed in good faith

13

by our heirs for ever. We have also granted to all freemen of our kingdom, for us and our heirs forever, all the underwritten liberties, to be held and held by them and their heirs, of us and our heirs forever.

If any of our earls or barons, or others holding of us in chief by military service shall have died, and at the time of his death his heir shall be full of age and owe "relief" he shall have his inheritance on payment of the ancient relief, namely the heir or heirs of an earl, £100 for a whole earl's barony; the heir or heirs of a baron, £100 for a whole barony; the heir or heirs of a knight, 100s. at most for a whole knight's fee; and whoever owes less let him give less, according to the ancient custom of fiefs. If, however, the heir of any one of the aforesaid has been under age and in wardship, let him have his inheritance without relief and without fine when he comes of age.

The guardian of the land of an heir who is thus under age, shall take from the land of the heir nothing but reasonable produce, reasonable customs, and reasonable services, and that without destruction or waste of men or goods; and if we have committed the wardship of the lands of any such minor to the sheriff, or to any other who is responsible to us for its issues, and he has made destruction or waste of what he holds in wardship, we will take of him amends, and the land shall be committed to two lawful and discreet men of that fee, who shall be responsible for the issues to us or to him to whom we shall assign them; and if we have given or sold the wardship of any such land to anyone and he has therein made destruction or waste, he shall lose that wardship, and it shall be transferred to two lawful and discreet men of that fief, who shall be responsible to us in like manner as aforesaid.

The guardian, moreover, so long as he has the wardship of the land, shall keep up the houses, parks, fishponds, stanks, mills, and other things pertaining to the land, out of the issues of the same land; and he shall restore to the heir, when he has come to full age, all his land, stocked with ploughs and wainage, according as the seaon of husbandry shall require, and the issues of the land can reasonably bear.

Heirs shall be married without disparagement, yet so that before the marriage takes place the nearest in blood to that heir shall have notice.

A widow, after the death of her husband, shall forthwith and without difficulty have her marriage portion and inheritance; nor shall she give anything to her dower, or for her marriage portion, or for the inheritance which her husband and she held on the day of the death of that husband; and she may remain in the house of her husband for forty days after his death, within which time her dower shall be assigned to her.

No widow shall be compelled to marry, so long as she prefers to live without a husband; provided always that she gives security not to marry without our consent, if she holds of us, or without the consent of the lord of whom she holds, if she holds of another.

Neither we nor our bailiffs shall seize any land or rent for any debt, so long as the chattels of the debtor are sufficient to repay the debt; nor shall the sureties of the debtor be distrained so long as the principal debtor is able to satisfy the debt; and if the principal debtor shall fail to pay the debt, having nothing wherewith to pay it, then the sureties shall answer for the debt; and let them have the lands and rents of the debtor, if they desire them, until they are indemnified for the debt which they have paid for him, unless the principal debtor can show proof that he is discharged thereof as against the said sureties.

If one who has borrowed from the Jews any sum, great or small, die before that loan be repaid, the debt shall not bear interest while the heir is under age, of whomsoever he may hold; and if the debt fall into our hands, we will not take anything except the principal sum contained in the bond.

And if anyone die indebted to the Jews, his wife shall have her dower and pay nothing of that debt; and if any children of the deceased are left under age, necessaries shall be provided for them in keeping with the holding of the deceased; and out of the residue the debt shall be paid, reserving, however, service due to feudal lords; in like manner let it be done touching debts due to others than Jews.

No scutage nor aid shall be imposed on our kingdom, unless by common counsel of our kingdom, except for ransoming our person, for making our eldest son a knight, and for once marrying our eldest daughter; and for these there shall not be levied more than a reasonable aid. In like manner it shall be done concerning aids from the city of London.

And the city of London shall have all its ancient liberties

15

and free customs, as well by land as by water; furthermore, we decree and grant that all other cities, boroughs, towns, and ports shall have their liberties and free customs.

And for obtaining the common counsel of the kingdom anent the assessing of an aid (except in the three cases aforesaid) or of a scutage, we will cause to be summoned the archbishops, bishops, abbots, earls, and greater barons, severally by our letters; and we will moreover cause to be summoned generally, through our sheriffs and bailiffs, all others who hold of us in chief, for a fixed date, namely, after the expiry of at least forty days, and at a fixed place; and in all letters of such summons we will specify the reason of the summons. And when the summons has thus been made, the business shall proceed on the day appointed, according to the counsel of such as are present, although not all who were summoned have come.

We will not for the future grant to any one licence to take an aid from his own free tenants, except to ransom his body, to make his eldest son a knight, and once to marry his eldest daughter; and on each of these occasions there shall be levied only a reasonable aid. No one shall be distrained for performance of greater service for a knight's fee, or for any other free tenement, than is due therefrom. Common pleas shall not follow our court, but shall be held in some fixed place.

Inquests of *novel disseisin*, of *mort d'ancestor*, and of *darrein presentment*, shall not be held elsewhere than in their own county-courts, and that in manner following, — We, or, if we should be out of the realm, our chief justiciar, will send two justiciars through every county four times a year, who shall, along with four knights of the county chosen by the county, hold the said assizes in the county court, on the day and in the place of meeting of that court. And if any of the said assizes cannot be taken on the day of the county court, let there remain of the knights and freeholders, who were present at the county court on that day, as many as may be required for the efficient making of judgments, according as the business be more or less.

A freeman shall not be amerced for a slight offence, except in accordance with the degree of the offence; and for a grave offence he shall be amerced in accordance with the gravity of the offence, yet saving always his livelihood; and a merchant in the same way, saving his merchandise; and a villein shall be amerced in the same way, saving his wainage — if they have fallen into our mercy: and none of the aforesaid amercements shall be imposed except by the oath of honest men of the neighbourhood.

Earls and barons shall not be amerced except through their peers, and only in accordance with the degree of the offence.

A clerk shall not be amerced in respect of his lay holding except after the manner of the others aforesaid; further, he shall not be amerced in accordance with the extent of his ecclesiastical benefice.

No village or individual shall be compelled to make bridges at river banks, except those who from of old were legally bound to do so.

No sheriff, constable, coroners, or others of our bailiffs, shall hold pleas of our Crown.

All counties, hundreds, wapentakes, and trithings (except our demesne manors) shall remain at the old rents, and without any additional payment.

If any one holding of us a lay fief shall die, and our sheriff or bailiff shall exhibit our letters patent of summons for a debt which the deceased owed to us, it shall be lawful for our sheriff or bailiff to attach and catalogue chattels of the deceased, found upon the lay fief, to the value of that debt, at the sight of law-worthy men, provided always that nothing whatever be thence removed until the debt which is evident shall be fully paid to us; and the residue shall be left to the executors to fulfil the will of the deceased; and if there be nothing due from him to us, all the chattels shall go to the deceased, saving to his wife and children their reasonable shares.

If any freeman shall die intestate, his chattels shall be distributed by the hands of his nearest kinsfolk and friends under supervision of the church, saving to every one the debts which the deceased owed to him.

No constable or other bailiff of ours shall take corn or other provisions from any one without immediately tendering money therefor, unless he can have postponement thereof by permission of the seller.

No constable shall compel any knight to give money in lieu of castleguard, when he is willing to perform it in his own person, or (if he himself cannot do it from any reasonable cause) then by another responsible man. Further, if we have led or sent him upon military service, he shall be relieved from guard in proportion to the time during which he has been on service because of us.

No sheriff or bailiff of ours, or other person, shall take the horses or carts of any freeman for transport duty, against the will of the said freeman.

Neither we nor our bailiffs shall take, for our castles or for any other work of ours, wood which is not ours, against the will of the owner of that wood.

We will not retain beyond one year and one day, the lands of those who have been convicted of felony, and the lands shall thereafter be handed over to the lords of the fiefs.

All fish-weirs for the future shall be removed altogether from Thames and Medway, and throughout all Engalnd, except upon the sea shore.

The writ which is called *praecipe* shall not for the future be issued to anyone, regarding any tenement whereby a freeman may lost his court.

Let there be one measure of wine throughout our whole realm; and one measure of ale; and one measure of corn, to wit, "the London quarter"; and one width of cloth (whether dyed, or russet, or "halberget"), to wit, two ells within the selvedges; of weights also let it be as of measures.

Nothing in future shall be given or taken for a writ of inquisition of life or limbs, but freely it shall be granted, and never denied. If anyone holds of us by fee-farm, by socage, or by burgage, and holds also land of another lord by knight's service, we will not (by reason of that fee-farm, socage, or burgage,) have the wardship of the heir, or of such land of his as is of the fief of that other; nor shall we have wardship of that fee-farm, socage, or burgage, unless such fee-farm owes knight's service. We will not by reason of any small serjeanty which anyone may hold of us by the service of rendering to us knives, arrows, or the like, have wardship of his heir or of the land which he holds of another lord by knight's service.

No bailiff for the future shall, upon his own unsupported complaint, put anyone on trial, without credible witnesses brought for this purpose.

No freeman shall be taken or imprisoned or disseised or outlawed or exiled or in any way destroyed, nor will we go upon him nor send upon him, except by the lawful judgment of his peers or by the law of the land.

To no one will we sell, to no one will we refuse or delay, right or justice.

All merchants shall have safe and secure exit from England, and entry to England, with the right to tarry there and to move about as well by land as by water, for buying and selling by the ancient and right customs, quit from all evil tolls, except (in time of war) such merchants as are of the land at war with us. And if such are found in our land at the beginning of the war, they shall be detained, without injury to their bodies or goods, until information be received by us, or. by our chief justiciar, how the merchants of our land found in the land at war with us are treated; and if our men are safe there, the others shall be safe in our land.

It shall be lawful in future for any one (excepting always those imprisoned or outlawed in accordance with the law of the kingdom, and natives of any country at war with us, and merchants, who shall be treated as is above provided) to leave our kingdom and to return, safe and secure by land and water, except for a short period in time of war, on grounds of public policy — reserving always the allegiance due to us.

If anyone holding of some escheat (such as the honour of Wallingford, Nottingham, Boulogne, Lancaster, or of other escheats which are in our hands and are baronies) shall die, his heir shall give no other relief, and perform no other service to us than he would have done to the baron, if that barony had been in the baron's hand; and we shall hold it in the same manner in which the baron held it.

Men who dwell without the forest need not henceforth come before our justiciars of the forest upon a general summons, except those who are impleaded, or who have become sureties for any person or persons attached for forest offences.

We will appoint as justices, constables, sheriffs, or bailiffs only such as know the law of the realm and mean to observe it well.

All barons who have founded abbeys, concerning which they hold charters from the kings of England, or of which they have long-continued possession, shall have the wardship of them, when vacant, as they ought to have.

All forests that have been made such in our time shall forthwith be disafforested; and a similar course shall be followed with regard to river-banks that have been enclosed by us in our time.

All evil customs connected with forests and warrens, foresters and warreners, sheriffs and their officers, river-banks and their wardens, shall immediately be inquired into in each county by twelve sworn knights of the same county chosen by the honest men of the same county, and shall, within forty days of the said inquest, be utterly abolished, so as never to be restored, provided always that we previously have intimation thereof, or our justiciar, if we should not be in England.

We will immediately restore all hostages and charters delivered to us by Englishmen, as sureties of the peace or of faithful service.

We will entirely remove from their bailiwicks, the relations of Gerard of Athée (so that in future they shall have no bailiwick in England); namely, Engelard of Cigogné, Peter, Guy, and Andrew of Chanceaux, Guy of Cigogné, Geoffrey of Martigny with his brothers, Philip Mark with his brothers and his nephew Geoffrey, and the whole brood of the same.

As soon as peace is restored, we will banish from the kingdom all foreign-born knights, cross-bowmen, serjeants, and mercenary soldiers, who have come with horses and arms to the kingdom's hurt.

If any one has been dispossessed or removed by us, without the legal judgment of his peers, from his lands, castles, franchises, or from his right, we will immediately restore them to him; and if a dispute arise over this, then let it be decided by the five-and-twenty barons of whom mention is made below in the clause for securing the peace. Moreover, for all those possessions, from which any one has, without the lawful judgment of his peers, been disseised or removed, by our father, King Henry, or by our brother, King Richard, and which we retain in our hand (or which are possessed by others, to whom we are bound to warrant them) we shall have respite until the usual term of crusaders; excepting those things about which a plea has been raised, or an inquest made by our order, before our taking of the cross; but as soon as we return from our expedition (or if perchance we desist from the expedition) we will immediately grant full justice therein. We shall have, moreover, the same respite and in the same manner in rendering justice concerning the disafforestation or retention of those forests which Henry our father and Richard our brother afforested, and concerning the wardship of lands which are of the fief of another (namely, such wardships as we have hitherto had by reason of a fief which anyone held of us by knight's service), and concerning abbeys founded on other fiefs than our own, in which the lord of the fee claims to have right; and when we have returned, or if we desist from our expedition, we will immediately grant full justice to all who complain of such things.

No one shall be arrested or imprisoned upon the appeal of a woman, for the death of any other than her husband.

All fines made with us unjustly and against the law of the land, and all amercements imposed unjustly and against the law of the land, shall be entirely remitted, or else it shall be done concerning them according to the decision of the five-and-twenty barons of whom mention is made below in the clause for securing the peace, or according to the judgment of the majority of the same, along with the aforesaid Stephen, archbishop of Canterbury, if he can be present, and such others as he may wish to bring with him for this purpose, and if he cannot be present the business shall nevertheless proceed without him, provided always that if one or more of the aforesaid five-and-twenty barons are in a similar suit, they shall be removed as far as concerns this particular judgment, others being substituted in their places after having been selected by the rest of the same five-and-twenty for this purpose only, and after having been sworn.

If we have disseised or removed Welshmen from lands or liberties, or other things, without the legal judgment of their peers in England or in Wales, they shall be immediately restored to them; and if a dispute arise over this, then let it be decided in the marches by the judgment of their peers; for tenements in England according to the law of England, for tenements in Wales according to the law of Wales, and for tenements in the marches according to the law of the marches. Welshmen shall do the same to us and ours.

Further, for all those possessions from which any Welshmen

has, without the lawful judgment of his peers, been disseised by King Henry our father, or King Richard our brother, and which we retain in our hand (or which are possessed by others to whom we are bound to warrant them) we shall have respite until the usual term of crusaders; excepting those things about which a plea has been raised or an inquest made by our order before we took the cross; but as soon as we return, (or if perchance we desist from our expedition), we will immediately grant full justice in accordance with the laws of the Welsh and in relation to the aforesaid regions.

We will immediately give up the son of Llywelyn and all the hostages of Wales, and the charters delivered to us as security for the peace.

We will do towards Alexander, King of Scots, concerning the return of his sisters and his hostages, and concerning his franchises, and his right, in the same manner as we shall do towards our other barons of England, unless it ought to be otherwise according to the charters which we hold from William his father, formerly King of Scots; and this shall be according to the judgment of his peers in our court.

Moreover, all these aforesaid customs and liberties, the observance of which we have granted in our kingdom as far as pertains to us towards our men, shall be observed by all of our kingdom, as well clergy as laymen, as far as pertains to them towards their men.

Since, moreover, for God and the amendment of our kingdom and for the better allaying of the quarrel that has arisen between us and our barons, we have granted all these concessions, desirous that they should enjoy them in complete and firm endurance for ever, we give and grant to them the under-written security, namely, that the barons choose five-and-twenty barons of the kingdom, whomsoever they will, who shall be bound with all their might, to observe and hold, and cause to be observed, the peace and liberties we have granted and confirmed to them by this our present Charter, so that if we, or our justiciar, or our bailiffs or any one of our officers, shall in anything be at fault toward anyone, or shall have broken any one of the articles of the peace or of this security, and the offence be notified to four barons of the aforesaid five-and-twenty, the said four barons shall repair to us (or our justiciar, if we are out of the realm) and, laying the transgression before us, petition to have that transgression redressed without delay. And if we shall not have corrected the transgression (or, in the event of our being out of the realm, if our justiciar shall not have corrected it) within forty days, reckoning from the time it has been intimated to us (or to our justiciar, if we should be out of the realm), the four barons aforesaid shall refer that matter to the rest of the five-and-twenty barons, and those five-and-twenty barons shall, together with the community of the whole land, distrain and distress us in all possible ways, namely, by siezing our castles, lands, possessions, and in any other way they can, until redress has been obtained as they deem fit, saving harmless our own person, and the persons of our queen and children; and when redress has been obtained, they shall resume their old relations towards us. And let whoever in the country desires it, swear to obey the orders of the said five-and-twenty barons for the execution of all the aforesaid matters, and along with them, to molest us to the utmost of his power; and we publicly and freely grant leave to everyone who wishes to swear, and we shall never forbid anyone to swear. All those, moreover, in the land who of themselves and of their own accord are unwilling to swear to the twenty-five to help them in constraining and molesting us, we shall by our command compel the same to swear to the effect foresaid. And if any one of the five-and-twenty barons shall have died or departed from the land, or be incapacitated in any other manner which would prevent the foresaid provisions being carried out, those of the said twenty-five barons who are left shall choose another in his place according to their own judgment, and he shall be sworn in the same way as the others. Further, in all matters, the execution of which is intrusted to these twenty-five barons, if perchance these twenty-five are present and disagree about anything, or if some of them, after being summoned, are unwilling or unable to be present, that which the majority of those present ordain or command shall be held as fixed and established, exactly as if the whole twenty-five had concurred in this; and the said twenty-five shall swear that they will faithfully observe all that is aforesaid, and cause it to be observed with all their might. And we shall procure nothing from anyone, directly or indirectly, whereby any part of these concessions and liberties might be revoked or diminished; and if any such thing has been procured, let it be void and null, and we shall never use it personally or by another.

And all the ill-will, hatreds, and bitterness that have arisen between us and our men, clergy and lay, from the date of the quarrel, we have completely remitted and pardoned to everyone. Moreover, all trespasses occasioned by the said quarrel, from Easter in the sixteenth year of our reign till the restoration of peace, we have fully remitted to all, both clergy and laymen, and completely forgiven, as far as pertains to us. And, on his head, we have caused to be made for them letters testimonial patent of the lord Stephen, archbishop of Canterbury, of the bishops aforesaid, and of Master Pandulf as touching this security and the concessions aforesaid.

Wherefore it is our will, and we firmly enjoin, that the English Church be free, and that the men in our kingdom have and hold all the aforesaid liberties, rights, and concessions, well and peacably, freely and quietly, fully and wholly, for themselves and their heirs, of us and our heirs, in all respects and in all places for ever, as is aforesaid. An oath, moreover, has been taken, as well on our part as on the part of the barons, that all these conditions aforesaid shall be kept in good faith and without evil intent. Given under our hand — the above-named and many others being witnesses — in the meadow which is called Runnymede, between Windsor and Staines, on the fifteenth day of June, in the seventeenth year of our reign.